the tournaments 6

66666

the tournaments

by Paul J. Deegan
illustrated by Harold Henriksen

AMECUS STREET, MANKATO, MINNESOTA

Published by Amecus Street, 123 South Broad Street, P.O. Box 113, Mankato, Minnesota 56001.
Copyright © 1975 by Amecus Street. International copyright reserved in all countries.
No part of this book may be reproduced in any form without written permission from the publisher.
Printed in the United States.

Library of Congress Number: 74-14936   ISBN: 0-87191-404-2
Library of Congress Cataloging in Publication Data
Deegan, Paul J   1937-
The tournaments.
(His A Dan Murphy story)
SUMMARY: In his senior year at Kennedy High, Dan Murphy helps his basketball team get to the state tournament finals.
(1. Basketball—Fiction) I. Keely, John, illus. II. Title.
PZ7.D359To   (Fic.)   74-14936   ISBN 0-87191-404-2

6666

Dan Murphy grabbed a towel off the dugout bench and wiped his face. It wasn't so hot on this late August day, but he had been working hard. His Pinetown American Legion baseball team was in the finals of the regional Legion tournament and Dan was pitching.

Only Pinetown and New Berlin were left of the champions from six states who had started in the tournament earlier in the week. Pinetown had been beaten once. New Berlin was unbeaten. It took two losses to put a team out of the tournament. If Pinetown lost, they went home and New Berlin advanced to the national tournament.

It was the bottom of the fifth inning of the seven-inning game. The score was tied 1-1. Dan was pitching well but so was the boy from New Berlin. Dan, who would be a 12th grader when school began in a couple weeks, was over 6 feet, 4 inches tall. He had also gained strength and weight over the summer. This had helped him become a more effective pitcher.

Dan had considered giving up baseball at one time. Basketball was his first sport. He spent some time nearly every day of the year with a basketball. He figured he had a good chance to play the sport in college. He didn't want anything, even baseball — which he enjoyed, to interfere with this goal.

Yet here he was, late in the summer, concentrating on baseball. The Pinetown Legion coach, Pat Harder, had very much wanted Dan to pitch for the team this year. Dan had been a good enough pitcher on the Kennedy High School team for two years and last summer with the Legion. Mr. Harder, though, had guessed that Dan, a left-hander, would be much better this summer as he physically approached manhood.

He had been right. Dan's fast ball was much improved. He could throw it right past many opponents. His previous successes in baseball and basketball had increased his confidence. He had a winning attitude. Dan would seldom beat himself. If in trouble, he would not ease a pitch up to the plate, hoping the batter might not bang it out. Dan would challenge the batter with his fastball or his still unpolished curve.

Pinetown had failed to put anyone on base. It was time for Dan to go back to the mound for the top of the sixth inning. He completed his warmup tosses quickly and looked at the batter stepping into the box. He was the eighth batter in the New Berlin lineup. Dan had noticed earlier that this hitter was not very quick with the bat.

Dan threw a fast ball by him for the

strike and came back with another fast ball. The batter swung a bit late and pushed a medium-hard ball to the Pinetown second baseman who had the easy play.

The ninth batter for New Berlin was a small guy. Their center fielder, he was very fast and had earlier tried to bunt for a hit. Dan threw a wide-breaking pitch which caught the inside of the plate for a strike. He came back with a fast ball, which he tried to get inside but which hopped over the middle of the plate. The batter fouled it back. Dan came back with another fast ball, kept it low, and got a called third strike.

That brought up the New Berlin leadoff hitter. Fairly tall and slender, he took a good swing and had hit safely once before, scoring his team's only run.

Dan paused for a second. He wanted to pitch carefully to this boy. Dan threw a good fast ball which was fouled off into the stands. He threw a curve, which missed for a ball. He came back with a fast ball which was rapped sharply to the left side of the infield. The Pinetown shortstop made a good play and threw out the batter by a step.

One more inning to go — if Pinetown could score this time. Dan would be up second. In the dugout he toweled off his face and arms and went to the on-deck circle where he watched the first man up strike out.

Dan took his stance in the left-handed batter's box. His stance was slightly open, his right foot turned toward the first base line. He stood fairly deep in the box, somewhat back from the plate. His size enabled him to stand away and still cover the plate with his swing.

Dan checked his swing on the first pitch, a curve from the New Berlin right-hander. It was a good pitch, right at the knees, and the umpire called "Ste-er-rike." The pitcher tried another breaking pitch and missed.

Dan thought the pitcher would now try to get ahead in the count by throwing his fast ball. Dan cocked his bat, watched the ball leave the pitcher's hand, and saw that it was coming straight and away and low. Dan flexed his knees slightly more than usual, got his weight out in front, and timed his swing well. The contact of bat on ball felt solid and he moved quickly out of the batter's box.

Racing toward first base, he saw the ball heading toward right center. It was too far from the New Berlin right fielder, who was running toward it, for him to make the catch. The center fielder was hustling and might make the catch. He didn't make it to the ball and it crashed against the fence on the first bounce. Dan rounded first hard and went into second standing up.

John Philips, the Pinetown left fielder, was the next batter. He took the first pitch to him for a ball and then popped the ball into short left field. The New Berlin shortstop went back and made the catch. Dan had to stay at second.

He clapped his hands and shouted encouragement at Mike O'Brien as the Pinetown first baseman moved to the plate. "He's got to come through," Dan thought to himself. "We may not get a chance like this again."

O'Brien let the first pitch go by for a ball. He fouled the second pitch into the

dirt. Dan had taken good leads on both pitches. He noticed that the New Berlin shortstop was playing very deep against the right-handed hitting O'Brien. On neither pitch had the New Berlin second baseman come over to make Dan hurry back to second.

On the third pitch Dan kept moving. He was one-third of the way down the line toward third base when O'Brien hit the ball on the ground between first and second. Dan kept going. Head up as he neared third, he saw Mr. Harder waving him on. He hit the inside of the third base bag and dug hard for home.

Dan knew that O'Brien's ball had not been hit very hard and he expected a play at the plate. As he approached home, the New Berlin catcher was crouched for a throw. The Pinetown on-deck batter was motioning with his arms and yelling, "Down!" Dan started his slide and went behind the catcher who had to reach forward for the bouncing ball thrown from right field. Pinetown was ahead, 2-1.

Dan bounced up and ran to the

dugout where his teammates greeted him with outstretched palms. He had barely sat down when a third strike was called on the Pinetown hitter. Out to the mound he went with only one thing in mind — to get the game over quickly.

And he did. Six pitches later, he had recorded a routine fly ball to right, a bouncer back to himself, and an easy ground ball to second for the final out.

Pinetown was still alive in the tournament, and Dan was being mobbed by his teammates.

However, the thrill didn't last even to the end of the day. In the championship game, New Berlin hammered three Pinetown pitchers for eight runs; the three Pinetown runs weren't nearly enough.

"Actually there wasn't too much disappointment," Dan was explaining to Sandra Brady a few days later. Dan and Sandra had been going out together since they had been in 10th grade. "None of us really expected to go that far anyway and it was hard to realize that we were really going after a place in the national tournament.

"New Berlin had a fine team and I think we all sort of letdown after beating them the first time in such a close game. It's always nice to win but with school only a few days away I'm kinda glad we're through playing baseball."

"Yeh, now you can start thinking about basketball again . . . if you ever stopped," Sandra said.

"Well, I wasn't thinking about it when I was pitching in that tournament," Dan said. "But I did take a basketball along and even got in some shooting on a couple of days that we were there."

"I'm not surprised," Sandra said. "I know you like being with me, but I'm not sure I come ahead of basketball."

"Oh, they're two different things," Dan said. "You're a person, and basketball's a game. People are important but I like to compete, too, and basketball's where I've done best. It's a nice feeling, knowing that you're good at something."

"The team will be good, too, won't it?" Sandra asked.

"Yeh, we should be," Dan replied.

"We've got four starters back and we did pretty well last year. We got beat out in the tournaments right away. That shouldn't happen again this season with our experience.

"The guys are working hard, too. Jake Tolson has spent more time on basketball this summer than ever before. He's also worked on weights some and should be a lot stronger. He's 6 feet 8 but he might play against some taller guys. There shouldn't be any that he can't handle, though.

"Have you seen Stan Sterner lately?" Dan asked. "He's grown a couple inches. He's probably over 6 feet 5. He can really get up, too. He's the best jumper I've seen around.

"This summer I've played a lot with Greg Sims, too. He's got much more confidence now in his shooting and moves. He'll score quite a bit more this year."

"Who will be your fifth starter?" Sandra asked.

"I'm not sure," Dan said, "but if I had to guess right now, I'd say Willie Johnson."

"You mean the tall, black kid that played on the 10th grade team last year?" Sandra asked.

"Yeh," Dan said. "There were three better-than-average players on the 10th grade team last year, but Willie was the best. He's not that tall — about 6 foot 2 — but he's very quick and has improved his shooting this summer. He's played with us several times in the evening."

"I sure hope you guys do well," Sandra said. "I don't think the football team is going to be too great. It'll be nice to be a cheerleader for a team that's winning."

Dan smiled and said, "You're just thinking about yourself. You don't really care about us guys or the school. You just want to be around a winner."

"What's so bad about that, Dan Murphy?" Sandra asked. "You don't seem to enjoy losing that much yourself!"

"I guess you're right about that," Dan said. "I have to give you a bad time about something, though. If we don't fight sometimes, people will think we're serious about each other."

"From what I've seen of married people," Sandra said, "those that never argue about anything may be the ones that aren't serious. I don't see how two people can always agree on everything, even if they are married or in love or whatever."

"Welcome to the Sandra Brady course on marriage," Dan said, again smiling.

"Somebody has to broaden your interests, Dan. There are some hours in the day or year when you can't be playing basketball or baseball."

"Oh, I've got other interests," Dan said.

"Name one besides me," Sandra replied.

"Who said you were one of them?" Dan said, laughing and moving back in case Sandra decided to take a swipe at him.

The following week, Dan, Sandra, and their classmates began their final year at Kennedy, one of Pinetown's two senior high schools. Even though Sandra gave Dan a bad time about his interest in sports, he actually enjoyed school. He liked most of his classes and was a good student. He had just under an A average for his first three years of high school.

Sandra's marks were a little better, something she reminded him about sometimes when they talked about their futures. "I might want to be a doctor," Sandra had said once. "But what if I go to school for several years and start a career? Would my husband, if I get married, expect me to form my life around his career? Would that be fair?"

Dan didn't really know how to answer the question. It certainly seemed right that if a woman was a doctor — or a teacher or whatever — she should be able to continue her work.

Yet Dan knew that his mother had quit teaching shortly after marrying Mr. Murphy. Most of her time was spent at home. Dan's sister, Sheila, was now in college and a younger brother, Jack, was in eighth grade.

Dan hadn't heard his mother complain about her role. She seemed satisfied. Yet he knew that not every woman felt the

same way. He had heard his parents speak about some of their friends who were having problems because the wife was no longer satisfied just taking care of the house and the children.

His parents seemed to understand what these women were saying. "There's a lot more opportunity for satisfaction in what I do," Dan recalled his father saying. Mr. Murphy was a vice-president of the Pinetown National Bank.

"Anybody's job requires him or her to do many unexciting things," Mr. Murphy had said. "But we men often get recognition for doing something well. Those of us who like dealing with people get that everyday, too. It's not often that someone tells a housewife that she really did a good job cleaning the house. Unless she leaves the house, she doesn't get much chance to meet people either."

One of the topics in a 12th grade social problems course was going to be the role of women in today's society. Dan was looking forward to those class discussions.

The fall days seemed to go more

quickly than the long summer days just passed. After classes, Dan and several teammates would go to the gym. The coaches couldn't start basketball practice until November. Almost every day, though, the guys who expected to play for the varsity would work out.

If the weather was decent, they would sometimes gather again at night on a lighted court at a city park for another hour of basketball.

Dan, who had been chosen captain of the team the preceding spring, noticed that his classmates seemed more serious in the workouts. There wasn't as much fooling around as there had been the previous year. When someone made a misplay, he was likely to be chewed out by another guy.

The team knew they could be good. They also knew it would take a serious effort by everybody to produce an outstanding season.

When practice officially started, Kennedy Stags' Coach Al McNulty spent the first days of practice stressing conditioning. "If we get beat," he told the team, "I don't want it to be because we ran out of gas in the last quarter. We want to be able to play hard in the final minutes just as we do at the beginning of a game."

After each practice in the first week, Dan led his teammates as they ran around the gym 20 times — a mile. Dan had been running outside during the summer, but the mile run after a hard workout was tough. He had to go all out to finish the 20 laps on the first couple of days.

Coach McNulty had decided the team not only had good size but was also fairly quick. So he spent a lot of time working on a pressing defense. After 20 minutes straight of playing a full-court press, even a boy in good shape welcomed a breather.

The press was designed to trap the man with the ball. The defense hoped to force the ball-handler into a bad pass which they might have a good chance to pick off.

Dan was not only tall but in the last few months he had developed good quickness. He was the last man in the pressing defense. He had to handle a breakaway if the defense broke down. He also was responsible for instructing the other four players where to go as the ball came up court. He had enough natural ability and experience to feel confident in this job.

The first test of the pressing defense came in the season's opener against Fort Harwood. The Kennedy players were really glad to see the season start. They had been looking forward to it for a long time and had had enough of practice. They wanted to play someone.

Coach McNulty kept the Stags in a normal man-to-man defense for the first quarter. At the quarter break, which saw Kennedy in a six-point lead, the coach told his team to put on the press.

It broke down the first time and Fort Harwood got a two-man break against Dan. He forced the man with the ball into making his move a little early. The opposing player put up a shot from too far out and missed.

The next time down, Fort Harwood threw the ball away. Two interceptions and a ball-handling violation followed and Kennedy opened up the score. They led by 16 at halftime and never went back to the press in the easy victory.

Kennedy also won their next six games, entering the Christmas vacation period undefeated. Dan was averaging 20 points a game and everyone else was making a contribution. Jake Tolson was scoring more than he ever had before, including 26 in one game. Stan Sterner was a terror, crashing the boards from his wing position. Greg Sims was scoring well from his low post or baseline spot in Kennedy's 1-2-2 offense. Willie Johnson had taken over the other wing post early in pre-season practice. His speed was a welcome addition to the starting five.

The Stags kept winning.

They were 18 and 0 near the end of February and not only the school but most of the community, including fans of rival Roosevelt High, were excited about the team.

Two games remained on the regular season's schedule. The first one was win number 19 by a comfortable margin. That left a Friday game at Albertville.

Kennedy had beaten this conference rival easily earlier in the year. Coach Mc-

Nulty knew that his players were going into the game overconfident. The conference title was already theirs. The coach tried hard to warn the team that Albertville had improved since their first meeting.

Right now, though, the Kennedy players figured nobody could beat them.

They were correct in a way. Despite improvement, Albertville was not good enough to beat the Stags. It took an assist from the Kennedy players to do that. They were awful in their final scheduled game.

Dan couldn't find the range from the field. Stan Sterner had trouble holding on to the ball. He also spent several minutes on the bench after picking up his third and fourth fouls on careless moves. Jake Tolson seemed frozen to one spot on the floor for most of the first three quarters. Greg Sims had trouble all night on defense against Albertville's best player, a rangy, quick forward. Only Willie Thompson played his normal game, but it wasn't enough to make up for the letdown by the rest of the starters.

With Kennedy down by 14 points midway in the third quarter, Coach Mc-

Nulty went to his bench and worked three other players into the game at various times. This seemed to shake the starting five out of their trance a bit, but they still trailed by six points with three minutes to play.

After signaling for a time-out, Coach McNulty put his starting five back on the floor. "Nobody's played well except Willie," he told the team. "There's not much time left, but you could still win this game. You're good enough. Let's play basketball for three minutes. Go into the full-court press."

Dan took the ball to the top of the circle, dribbled down to his left, then cut back hard to his right. The move left him free for a jump shot. He went up and put the ball through the hoop.

Thompson and Sterner trapped the Albertville player who took the inbounds pass. He was in trouble and Dan anticipated where he would try to pass. Dan left his position and was moving toward the pass before it was released. He beat the Albertville boy who was coming back for the ball, grabbed it, and noticed Jake Tolson moving toward the basket. A quick pass to Jake produced a lay-up.

The Albertville player who was to pass in the ball decided this time to go to a teammate coming from the center-court area. Tolson tipped the pass-in, and Thompson picked it up. He drove to the basket, went behind the glass board, and put in a reverse lay-up.

The score was tied with a minute and 45 seconds to play. Albertville got the ball in bounds after taking a time-out and brought it into their front-court. They were going to go for a good shot. Kennedy was playing good defense and the clock went down to 20 seconds when Albertville called another time-out.

"Don't foul and don't let them get inside," Coach McNulty told the Kennedy players.

Albertville hadn't been able to get a good shot when only four seconds remained on the scoreboard. From 25 feet out, an Albertville player launched a desperation shot. The ball bounced high off the back rim and seemed to hang in the air for minutes. Then it dropped back down and through the net.

The game was over. The Stags were no longer undefeated.

It was very quiet in the Kennedy locker room. A few profanities broke the silence. The four players who hadn't played went to the shower room. The others sat in front of the lockers. All wished they had the game to play over.

"Okay, forget it," Coach McNulty said as he walked to where his players were sitting. "It was nice to be undefeated but we had a great season. At least you know now that you're not unbeatable. I'm not sure why no one except Willie played ball until the final minutes, but we didn't.

"We had a good comeback and got beat on a lucky shot. But if we'd played halfway decent earlier, we wouldn't have been in trouble.

"You've learned how to win this year; now let's see you be graceful in defeat. You don't have to like it, but it's over. I want you to walk out of here with your heads high. You're still conference champions. Sulking won't change tonight's score. Take out your disappointment in the tournaments."

The Stags did come back strong in tournament play. They won their first three games by margins of 15, 20, and 18 points. The feeling of superiority was returning. This time, though, it was tempered by the recognition that a letdown would bring defeat. And a defeat now would mean the end of their dream of a state championship.

Kennedy had two games to play to gain the sectional finals. They had gone to the finals two years ago when Dan was a 10th grader. He had moved up to the varsity late in the season when the first-string point man was injured. Dan had started the game which Kennedy lost in the sectional finals. He didn't want to lose there again.

First, though, the team had to make it to the big game, which would be played at Western University.

Kennedy scored a 10-point victory in their next tournament game. After trailing by four points at halftime two nights later, they put their game together in the second half and finished 12 points ahead of a strong Earnwell High team.

Now it was back to Schoolton and Western U for the sectional championship. The winner would be one of four teams going to the finals of the public school tournament at State University the following weekend.

Dan had been tense but not scared on the bus ride to Schoolton two years ago. This time he was quite confident. The nerve-tingling tension was still present, however.

Dan knew his teammates too well to feel comfortable making speeches to them. Tonight, though, just before the team went back on the floor for the introductions, he asked Coach McNulty if he could say something.

"Sure, Dan, go ahead," the coach said.

"I'm not going to give you guys any baloney," Dan said. "You wouldn't believe it if I did. I just want to say that you and I know that we have a very good team... if we produce. As you know, I was here once before. We lost that night. I want to walk out of this room two hours from now a winner. Let's take it to them."

Kennedy played with a quiet confidence. Their play seemed to tell the opposing Forest River players: "We know we're going to win, and it really doesn't make much difference what you do."

Forest River would put together a good series, and Kennedy would come back with a better one. Forest River would score off a break, and Kennedy would get two fast breaks. Dan and Jake felt they could score any time they had the ball. They almost did. At the half, Kennedy had shot an unbelievable 70 per cent from the field. They had made 22 of 31 field goal attempts and led, 49-35. Dan had 18 points and Jake 15 at halftime.

They couldn't keep up the same precision in the second half, but Kennedy kept enough margin so that Coach McNulty was able to remove his starters midway through the fourth period.

When Dan sat down on the bench after exchanging hand-slaps with his teammates, he noticed a big sign being held up across the floor. Sandra Brady was holding one end of the sign; another Kennedy cheerleader, the other. The sign read: "Kennedy Stags Are No. 1."

"Maybe we're not yet," Dan thought, "but by next Saturday night we could be."

Dan had trouble concentrating on his classes the following week. Everyone was talking about the state tournament finals. The team left Thursday morning so they would get in a workout on the State University Coliseum floor late that afternoon.

As Dan left his house that morning, his parents wished him luck. "Remember, Dan," his father said, "you've had a great season. Do your best but if you should lose, act like a champion."

"Sheila called last night and said she was coming to the games," his mother said. "We'll see you sometime tomorrow. I hope you come back with the championship. Remember, though, that very few players even get to the finals."

Kennedy faced Metro Westend in the first game on Friday. It was the first time all year that they had played a team who could match them overall in size. Westend also had a 6-foot, 11-inch center.

The Stags got off to a slow start, but their ability began to show late in the first quarter. Jake Tolson played his best game of the year and took his bigger opponent apart, blocking him off the boards so the other Kennedy players could go for the rebounds. Jake scored 28 points. Dan had 18 points and Greg Sims scored 14 as Kennedy captured a 75-66 victory to gain the state finals.

Their opponents on Saturday afternoon were the Huntley East Flyers. Huntley was undefeated and the favorite to win the tournament. They weren't quite as big as Kennedy but were somewhat faster. They pressed and favored a fast-breaking, free-lancing offense.

The Kennedy players knew they could be beaten but believed it could happen only if they beat themselves. They had done that once this year and weren't about to repeat the mistake.

The game was a great high school contest. Midway in the fourth quarter, the score was tied 64-64. Then Dan popped a 16-foot jumper off a screen by Tolson. When the Flyers came up court, Dan slapped the ball away from his man who had become careless for a moment about his dribble. Dan rushed after the ball, picked it up, and headed for the basket. He went behind his back to beat a slightly off-balance East player who had rushed back down court, then went over the rim to drop down a lay-up.

Seconds later, Stan Sterner leaped high to block a close-in Flyer scoring attempt. Jake picked up the loose ball and fired a perfect pass to the streaking Willie Thompson, who scored.

These six points broke open the game. A few minutes later, Dan was heading to the center of the floor to accept the state championship trophy as captain of the Kennedy team. After he received the large trophy, he waved to his teammates to join him.

As he stood under the scoreboard, which read "Kennedy 78, East 73," a Kennedy cheerleader ran over and gave him a big kiss. The name on her sweater was "Sandra."

DAN MURPHY SPORTS STORIES

CREATIVE EDUCATION

56123

THE TOURNAMENTS
THE TEAM MANAGER
IMPORTANT DECISION

DAN MOVES UP
ALMOST A CHAMPION
CLOSE BUT NOT QUITE